WITHDRAWN

# SPACE MYSTERIES

# WHAT IS AN ECLIPSE?

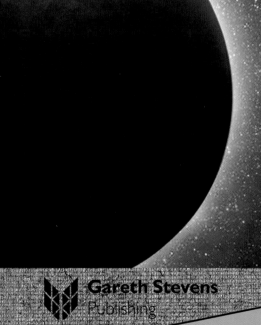

 Gareth Stevens
Publishing

BY MICHAEL PORTMAN

Please visit our website, www.garethstevens.com. For a free color catalog of all our high-quality books, call toll free 1-800-542-2595 or fax 1-877-542-2596.

**Library of Congress Cataloging-in-Publication Data**

Portman, Michael.
What is an eclipse? / by Michael Portman.
  p. cm. —(Space mysteries)
Includes index.
ISBN 978-1-4339-9234-6 (pbk.)
ISBN 978-1-4339-9235-3 (6-pack)
ISBN 978-1-4339-9233-9 (library binding)
1. Solar eclipses—Juvenile literature. I. Portman, Michael, 1976- II. Title.
QB541.P67 2014
523.7'8—dc23

First Edition

Published in 2014 by
**Gareth Stevens Publishing**
111 East 14th Street, Suite 349
New York, NY 10003

Copyright © 2014 Gareth Stevens Publishing

Designer: Katelyn E. Reynolds
Editor: Therese Shea

Photo credits: Cover, p. 1 © iStockphoto.com/sdecoret; cover, pp. 1, 3–32 (background texture) David M. Schrader/Shutterstock.com; pp. 3–32 (fun fact graphic) © iStockphoto.com/spxChrome; pp. 5, 9 (lunar), 27 iStockphoto/Thinkstock.com; p. 7 Petar Milevski/Shutterstock.com; p. 9 (solar) Digital Vision/Thinkstock.com; p. 11 udaix/Shutterstock.com; p. 13 Comstock/Thinkstock.com; pp. 15, 25 Sagredo/Wikipedia.com; p. 17 Miloslav Druckmüller (Brno University of Technology), Martin Dietzel, Peter Aniol, Vojtech Rušin/NASA; p. 19 Alexander Chelmodeev/Shutterstock.com; p. 21 optimarc/Shutterstock.com; p. 23 Babak Tafreshi/Photo Researchers/Getty Images; p. 29 Antony Dickson/AFP/Getty Images.

Printed in the United States of America

CPSIA compliance information: Batch #CS13GS: For further information contact Gareth Stevens, New York, New York at 1-800-542-2595.

# CONTENTS

Constant Motion.................................................................. 4

Lining Up.......................................................................... 6

Types of Eclipses ............................................................... 8

New Moon ...................................................................... 10

Looks Can Deceive .......................................................... 12

Moon Shadows ................................................................ 14

Total Solar Eclipse............................................................ 16

Partial Solar Eclipse.......................................................... 18

Annular Solar Eclipse ....................................................... 20

Hybrid Solar Eclipse ......................................................... 22

Penumbral Lunar Eclipse ................................................... 24

Partial and Total Lunar Eclipse........................................... 26

When They Happen .......................................................... 28

Glossary.......................................................................... 30

For More Information ........................................................ 31

Index............................................................................... 32

Words in the glossary appear in **bold** type the first time they are used in the text.

# CONSTANT MOTION

Our **solar system** doesn't stand still. Earth, our moon, and all the planets are in constant motion. Earth spins, or rotates, on its **axis** once every 24 hours. It takes the moon a bit more than 27 days to circle, or orbit, Earth. Both Earth and the moon orbit the sun once every 365 days. These motions give us our days, months, and years.

During the journey around the sun, sometimes Earth, the moon, and the sun line up. This formation gives us the event called an eclipse.

The moon takes 27 days, 7 hours, 43 minutes, 11.6 seconds to orbit Earth.

**5**

# LINING UP

For the most part, our solar system is shaped like an oval. The planets orbit the sun in the same direction and on the same **plane**. It's almost as if they each have their own lane on a racetrack. But if this is the case, why don't we have an eclipse every month?

The moon's orbit is slightly **tilted**. That means the moon is usually too high or too low to line up with Earth and the sun.

## OUT OF THIS WORLD!

Because the moon's orbit is a bit tilted, it only comes directly between Earth and the sun about twice a year.

An eclipse is the total or partial covering of one space object by another.

7

# TYPES OF ECLIPSES

From Earth, we can see two kinds of eclipses: solar eclipses and lunar eclipses. A solar eclipse is when the moon passes between Earth and the sun, covering all or part of the sun's surface. A lunar eclipse occurs when Earth passes between the sun and the moon and casts a shadow on the moon's surface.

There are four types of solar eclipses: total, partial, annular, and **hybrid**. There are three types of lunar eclipses: total, partial, and penumbral.

## OUT OF THIS WORLD!

Lunar eclipses are more common than solar eclipses.

lunar eclipse

solar eclipse

9

# NEW MOON

You probably know the moon goes through different **phases** each month. This is because the moon doesn't create its own light. Instead, it reflects sunlight. As the moon orbits Earth, the amount we can see of the moon's lighted side changes.

A solar eclipse can only occur during the new moon phase. At this time, the moon is between Earth and the sun. The part of the moon **illuminated** by the sun is pointing away from Earth.

## OUT OF THIS WORLD!

Gibbous is a phase when the illuminated part of the moon is greater than half but not full.

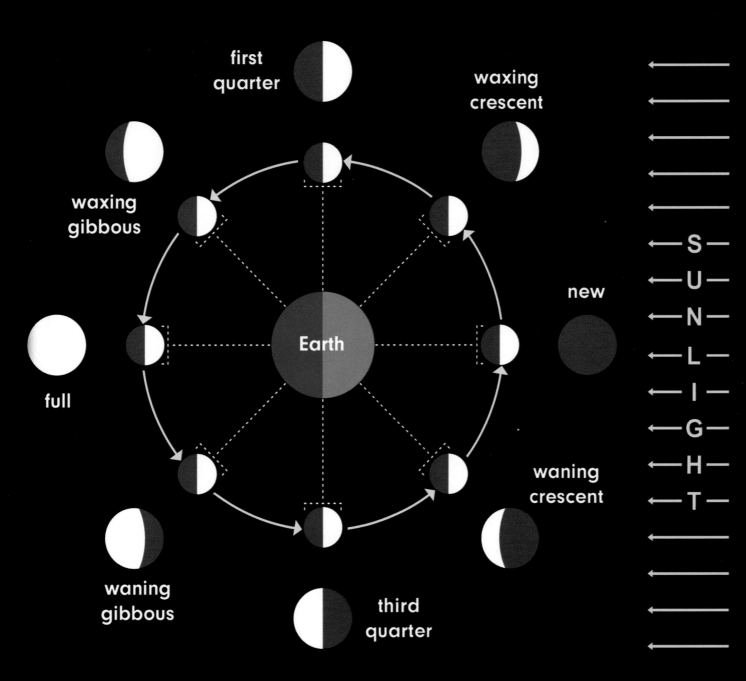

first quarter

waxing crescent

waxing gibbous

new

full

Earth

waning crescent

waning gibbous

third quarter

S
U
N
L
I
G
H
T

"Waxing" means the amount of the moon's illuminated surface we can see is increasing each night. "Waning" means it's decreasing.

11

# LOOKS CAN DECEIVE

Since the moon is relatively close to Earth, it can seem bigger than it actually is. In fact, the moon is at the perfect distance from Earth to appear exactly the same size as the sun.

The sun has a **diameter** of about 864,000 miles (1,390,000 km). That's 400 times greater than the diameter of the moon. And the moon just happens to be 400 times closer to Earth than the sun. If the moon were farther away, it wouldn't appear large enough to cover the sun.

The moon's diameter is about 2,160 miles (3,475 km). The sun is much, much larger.

moon

sun

# MOON SHADOWS

Everything orbiting the sun casts shadows through space. The moon casts two shadows on Earth during a solar eclipse. One shadow is called the umbra. It's the darkest shadow. The umbra narrows as it reaches Earth, somewhat like a cone. The second shadow, the penumbra, becomes wider as it reaches Earth.

Only those people living in the umbral shadow can see a total solar eclipse. People living in the penumbral shadow see a partial eclipse.

## OUT OF THIS WORLD!

Eclipse shadows move quickly—as fast as 5,000 miles (8,050 km) per hour near the North and South Poles!

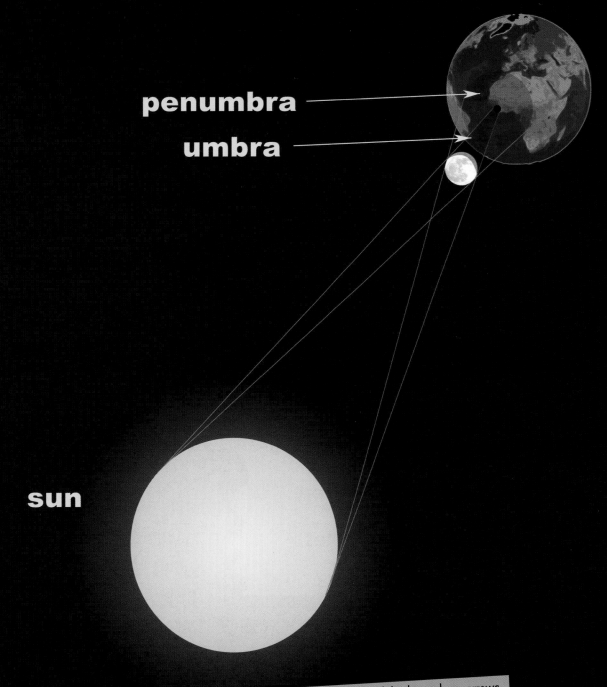

**penumbra**

**umbra**

**sun**

You can see in this diagram that the penumbra widens as it reaches Earth while the umbra narrows.

# TOTAL SOLAR ECLIPSE

A total solar eclipse occurs when the moon completely blocks the sun. The part of Earth covered by the umbra becomes dark like night, and the temperature drops. However, the sun's corona, or the outer layer of its atmosphere, is still visible.

A total eclipse happens about once every 18 months and can only be seen from a small part of Earth. It doesn't last very long, usually just a few minutes.

## OUT OF THIS WORLD!

During a total solar eclipse, the moon may block the sun as long as 7 minutes 30 seconds. However, the eclipse is usually quicker than this.

The period of totality is the time in which the sun is totally covered by the moon. The sun's corona is pictured here.

17

# PARTIAL SOLAR ECLIPSE

A partial solar eclipse occurs when the moon blocks only a part of the sun. It's visible on Earth to those in the penumbra. A partial eclipse may mean there's a total eclipse somewhere else on Earth, in the umbra. Or the umbra may have missed Earth altogether.

The closer a person lives to the umbra, the greater the amount of the sun that's blocked. Farther way, people see only a tiny sliver of the sun covered.

## OUT OF THIS WORLD!

The path of totality—the path the umbral shadow follows across Earth—is usually around 10,000 miles (16,100 km) long and about 100 miles (161 km) wide.

Partial eclipses are the most common type of solar eclipses.

19

# ANNULAR SOLAR ECLIPSE

An annular eclipse occurs when the moon is at its farthest distance from Earth. The moon doesn't have a perfectly circular orbit. Its distance from Earth can range from around 225,600 to 252,100 miles (363,000 to 405,630 km).

However, the moon's umbra **extends** 235,700 miles (379,240 km). If the moon is any farther from Earth than that, it looks too small to completely cover the sun. Instead, the sun appears as a ring of fire surrounding the moon. In fact, "annular" means "in the form of a ring."

**OUT OF THIS WORLD!**

An annular eclipse can last up to 12 minutes 30 seconds.

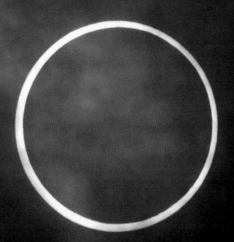

Since an annular solar eclipse doesn't cover as much of the sun, the sky doesn't darken much. This is a photo of an annular solar eclipse.

# HYBRID SOLAR ECLIPSE

A hybrid solar eclipse is a combination of an annular eclipse and a total eclipse. This happens when the moon's distance from Earth is equal to how far its umbra can reach.

Because Earth is round, a small part will touch the moon's umbra, but most of Earth will be too far away for the umbra to reach. Some areas experience a total eclipse, while others see an annular eclipse. A hybrid eclipse is the least common type of solar eclipse.

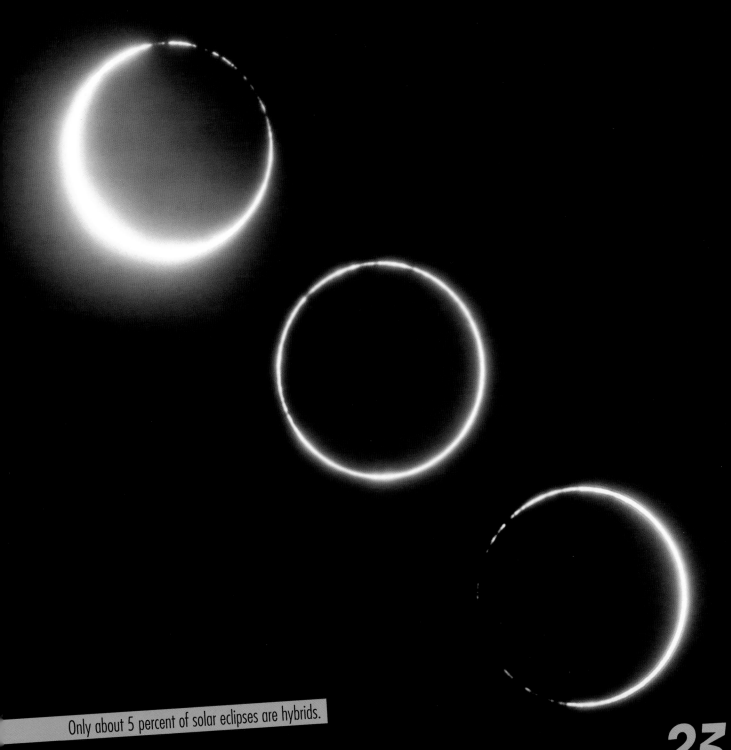

Only about 5 percent of solar eclipses are hybrids.

23

# PENUMBRAL LUNAR ECLIPSE

A lunar eclipse occurs when Earth comes between the sun and the moon. Earth casts its shadow on the moon. A lunar eclipse can only occur during a full moon, when the moon appears its biggest.

Like the moon, Earth casts two shadows: the penumbra and the umbra. The penumbral lunar eclipse is when the moon passes through Earth's penumbral shadow. This type of eclipse is very hard to see because the moon's surface only dims slightly.

**OUT OF THIS WORLD!**
*Umbra* is Latin for "shadow."

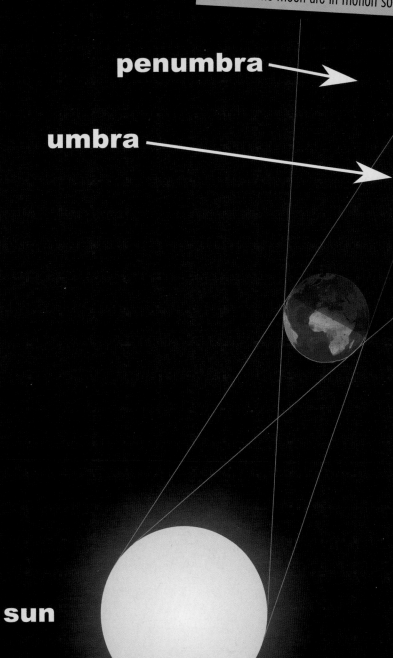

Earth and the moon are in motion so both shadows move quickly.

**penumbra** →

**umbra** →

**sun**

25

# PARTIAL AND TOTAL LUNAR ECLIPSE

A partial lunar eclipse occurs when only a portion of the moon passes through Earth's umbra. It appears as if something has taken a large bite out of the moon!

Finally, if Earth, the moon, and the sun are perfectly lined up, a total lunar eclipse occurs. The entire moon passes through Earth's dark umbral shadow. The moon dimly glows because of Earth's atmosphere. It might even be a dark red color!

When an eclipse of the moon occurs, everyone on the night side of Earth can see it.

27

# WHEN THEY HAPPEN

Eclipses aren't **random** events. A solar eclipse occurs at least twice and sometimes as many as five times a year. Three lunar eclipses may take place each year, too.

If you pay attention to the news or read space websites, you'll know when to expect one. You can safely look at lunar eclipses with your naked eyes, but <u>never</u> solar eclipses. Many people make or use special tools to get a safe view of a solar eclipse.

## OUT OF THIS WORLD!

Some people, called eclipse chasers, travel around the world to see total eclipses.

These people use specially made "solar viewers" to safely see a solar eclipse. Sunglasses aren't powerful enough.

29

# GLOSSARY

**axis:** an imaginary line around which a planet or moon turns

**diameter:** the distance from one side of a round object to another through its center

**extend:** to stretch out

**hybrid:** made up of two parts

**illuminate:** to light up

**phase:** a stage in a process or sequence of events

**plane:** a flat or level surface

**random:** occurring without a pattern or plan

**solar system:** the sun and all the space objects that orbit it, including the planets and their moons

**tilted:** slanted, not straight up and down

# FOR MORE INFORMATION

## BOOKS

James, Lincoln. *Solar Eclipses*. New York, NY: PowerKids Press, 2009.

Zappa, Marcia. *Eclipses*. Edina, MN: ABDO Publishing, 2011.

## WEBSITES

**Eclipse**
*education.nationalgeographic.com/education/encyclopedia/eclipse/?ar_a=4*
See amazing photos of all kinds of eclipses.

**Eclipses of the Sun & Moon Worldwide**
*www.timeanddate.com/eclipse/*
Find out when and where you can see an eclipse.

**How Solar Eclipses Work**
*science.howstuffworks.com/solar-eclipse.htm*
Read more about solar eclipses.

# INDEX

annular solar eclipse
8, 20, 21, 22

corona  16, 17

diameter  12, 13

eclipse chasers  28

full moon  24

hybrid solar eclipse
8, 22, 23

lunar eclipses  8, 9,
24, 26, 27, 28

new moon  10

orbit  4, 5, 6, 10, 14,
20

partial lunar eclipse
8, 26

partial solar eclipse
8, 14, 18, 19

path of totality  18

penumbra  8, 14, 15,
18, 24, 25

penumbral lunar
eclipse  8, 24

period of totality  17

phases  10

shadows  8, 14, 18,
24, 25, 26

solar eclipses  8, 9,
10, 14, 16, 18,
19, 21, 22, 23,
28, 29

solar system  4, 6

solar viewers  29

total lunar eclipse  8,
26

total solar eclipse  8,
14, 16, 18, 22

umbra  14, 15, 16, 18,
20, 22, 24, 25, 26